The Dash

To The Phyllis Nixon Family
May all your loving memories of your
mother and grandmother comfort and
carry you the days ahead.

From Suzanne & Doug Kibbe

DEDICATED TO THE LIFE OF

JOHN WILLIAM HICKS,

THE DASH BETWEEN

JUNE 12, 1930 - JULY 5, 2004.

DAD, I'LL LOVE YOU FOREVER.

LINDA

The Dash

Making a Difference with Your Life

~ ❦ ~

by Linda Ellis and Mac Anderson

Photo Credits:
Steve Terrill *(www.terrillphoto.com)* Front cover, and pages 9, 11, 12, 14, 16,
18, 20, 22, 24, 26, 28, 30, 32, 34, 36, 38, 42, 45, 48, 52, 55, 59, 66, 68, 72, 75,
78, 82, 83, 85, 86.
Bruce Heinemann *(www.theartofnature.com)* pages 71, 91.
Todd Reed *(www.toddreedphoto.com)* pages 80, 84.
Shutterstock and Thinkstock pages 92-135

Design: Rich Nickel
Editor: Jennifer Svoboda

Printed and bound in China

OGP 10 9 8 7 6 5 4 3

Table of Contents

~❦~ *Introduction*

I remember it like it was yesterday. I had received a handwritten note from Anna Lee Wilson, a Successories franchisee from Evansville, Indiana, and at the bottom of the note was a postscript that read: "I know you have inspirational poems, and this is my all-time favorite. It's titled, *The Dash*, by Linda Ellis."

Now, I can count on one hand how many times I've read something that stopped me in my tracks... words that bypassed the brain and went straight to the heart. This was one of those moments. I immediately thought... how could I use my talents to share these powerful, thought-provoking words with the rest of the world?

I contacted Linda Ellis, introduced myself, and told her how much I love her poem. She told me how, in one afternoon in 1996, she was inspired to write *The Dash*. Her life, she said, has not been the same since then. And it hasn't been for anyone who has ever read her powerful words either!

That conversation sparked our publication of *The Dash* in 2005. Since we started Simple Truths almost seven years ago, we've been blessed to publish over 100 inspirational books, written by some of the best authors in the world. But of all the books we've created, none have had the emotional response of *The Dash*.

How do we know? Because we've heard from thousands of people all over the world telling us how *The Dash* has touched their souls and changed the way they think about life.

That's what this Special Edition of *The Dash* is all about. It's to celebrate life! It's to thank all those wonderful people for sharing how *The Dash* has made a difference in their lives and to inspire you to make a difference with yours.

I invite you to experience the power of Linda's poem and the content of our original book. On page 92, you'll be able to enjoy some of the wonderful stories submitted by our readers about the impact the poem has had in their lives. I hope it'll inspire you to live your dash with passion!

Live with passion,

Mac Anderson
Founder, Successories and Simple Truths

The Dash

By Linda Ellis

I read of a man who stood to speak

at the funeral of a friend.

He referred to the dates on her tombstone

from the beginning…to the end.

He noted that first came the date of her birth

and spoke of the following date with tears,

but he said what mattered most of all...

was the dash between those years.

For that dash represents all the time

       that she spent alive on earth

    and now only those who loved her

know what that little line is worth.

For it matters not, how much we own,

the cars…the house…the cash…

What matters is how we live and love...

and how we spend our dash.

So think about this long and hard;

are there things you'd like to change?

For you never know how much time is left

that can still be rearranged.

If we could just slow down enough

to consider what's true and real…

and always try to understand

the way other people feel.

And be less quick to anger

and show appreciation more

and love the people in our lives...

like we've never loved before.

If we treat each other with respect

and more often wear a smile…

remembering that this special dash

might only last a little while.

So when your eulogy is being read…

with your life's actions to rehash...

would you be proud of the things they say...

about how you spent your dash?

The Dash

By Linda Ellis

I read of a man who stood to speak
at the funeral of a friend.
He referred to the dates on her tombstone
from the beginning…to the end.

He noted that first came the date of her birth
and spoke of the following date with tears,
but he said what mattered most of all
was the dash between those years.

For that dash represents all the time
that she spent alive on earth
and now only those who loved her
know what that little line is worth.

For it matters not, how much we own,
the cars…the house…the cash.
What matters is how we live and love
and how we spend our dash.

So think about this long and hard;
are there things you'd like to change?
For you never know how much time is left
that can still be rearranged.

If we could just slow down enough
to consider what's true and real
and always try to understand
the way other people feel.

And be less quick to anger
and show appreciation more
and love the people in our lives
like we've never loved before.

If we treat each other with respect
and more often wear a smile...
remembering that this special dash
might only last a little while.

So when your eulogy is being read
with your life's actions to rehash,
would you be proud of the things they say
about how you spent your dash?

How will you spend your Dash?

One of the most difficult lessons in life to learn is that…less, is usually more. And only as I've grown older, have I "gotten it." Focusing on your most important priorities, and continually removing the clutter, will be key to any true success in your life. That's what I love about this poem. In 239 words, it captures the "simple truths" of why we were put on this earth.

Sometimes, when you look through the lens of a camera, the image is blurred. However, with one small tweak of the lens, it can become crystal clear. For me, that's what can happen when combining a beautiful photograph with inspirational words…it can resonate with your imagination and bring the idea to life.

Within the words of this beautiful poem, I discovered a few simple truths that can make a difference in any life. I'd like to share them with you to help bring your "dash goals" into focus.

May you live your Dash with passion,

Mac Anderson

"If we could just *slow down*
enough to consider what's true and real…"

Slow Down

I once heard someone say, "We don't remember days; we remember moments." However, at today's hectic pace we often forget to savor small pleasures while we make big plans.

In the race to be better or best, we sometimes lose sight of "just being." And just being, just soaking in and savoring a beautiful moment, can provide some of life's greatest pleasures. A crackling fire on a cold winter night; a good book; a love letter from your spouse; a spectacular sunset; a great meal; or a timeless moment with your child or a friend…these moments, if we stop long enough to enjoy, are the essence of life.

Slow Down

I love to fish, especially for large-mouth bass. About three years ago, I was watching television late one night and got this crazy notion to go fishing in the lake behind my house. Of course, my wife thought I was nuts. It was almost midnight! I convinced her I was sane and took off. I walked out to a warm summer breeze and looked up at the starry sky and breathtaking full moon. I allowed my senses to soak in every second — the sweet smell of honeysuckle, the sound of every cricket and bullfrog, the moon's reflection dancing off the water — it was a perfect night.

After walking across a small field, I took out a flashlight and selected a lure. On my first cast, I reeled in a bass weighing over five pounds, one of the largest I had ever caught. I gently released it back into the water and continued my midnight adventure. During the next two hours, I caught seventeen bass, all between two and five pounds. Although I've fished for almost fifty years, no fishing memory can top that warm summer night.

Slow

But that night provided far more than a fishing memory. It was a life memory. It provided me a snapshot of what life could be like if I just slowed down enough to savor the moments. On my way back to the house, as I walked through the tall grass, I took one last look at the sky and stopped to say, "Thank you, God, for giving me this night."

Remember, it will only last for a little while…so savor the moments, savor the memories of your Dash.

"Every hour of every day is an unspeakably perfect miracle."

—Walt Whitman

"If we could just slow down enough
to consider what's *true and real*..."

True and Real

Knowing yourself, finding your true purpose in life, is the essence of true and real. "You have to be, before you do, to have lasting inner peace." In other words, making a living is not the same as making a life. Find what makes your heart sing and create your own music.

Many people work all their lives and dislike what they do for a living. In fact, I was astounded to see a recent *USA Today* survey that said 53 percent of people in the American workplace are unhappy with their jobs. Loving what you do is one of the most important keys to living a "true and real" Dash.

You can't fake passion. It is the fuel that drives any dream and makes you happy to be alive. However, the first step to loving what you do is to self analyze, to simply know what you love. We all have unique talents and interests, and one of life's greatest challenges is to match these talents with career opportunities that bring out the best in us. It's not easy — and sometimes we can only find it through trial and error — but it's worth the effort.

Ray Kroc, for example, found his passion when he founded McDonald's at the age of 52. He never "worked" another day of his life.

John James Audubon was unsuccessful for most of his life. He was a terrible businessman. No matter how many times he changed locations, changed partners, or changed businesses, he still failed miserably. Not until he understood that he must change himself did he have any shot at success.

And what changes did Audubon make? He followed his passion. He had always loved the outdoors and was an excellent hunter. In addition, he was a good artist and, as a hobby, would draw local birds.

Once he stopped trying to be a businessman and started doing what he loved to do, his life turned around. He traveled the country observing and drawing birds, and his art ultimately was collected in a book titled *Audubon's Birds of America*. The book earned him a place in history as the greatest wildlife artist ever. But more importantly, the work made him happy and provided the peace of mind he'd been seeking all his life.

"Throw your heart over the fence and the rest will follow."

— NORMAN VINCENT PEALE

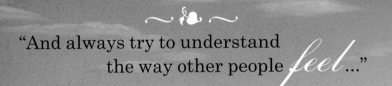

"And always try to understand
the way other people *feel*..."

Feelings

I once heard someone say, "If you teach your child the Golden Rule, you will have left them an incalculable estate." Truer words were never spoken.

More than anything, the Golden Rule is about kindness. As Mother Teresa said, "It's the only language that we all understand." John Blumberg, author, speaker and friend, recently told me a story that I'd like to share with you:

Feelings

Feelings

"I had just experienced a pleasant flight from New York back to Chicago on United Airlines. It was one of those days where almost everything had gone right. That's until I exited the tram to the airport's economy parking lot and realized that I had lost my wallet on my homeward journey.

Throughout the drive home I mentally started retracing my steps. Once home, I placed calls to the "lost-and-found" at O'Hare, United, NY-LaGuardia and the TSA security in New York. At that late night hour I got recordings, so I left each a detailed message. I then retired to bed knowing I had done all I could do. I fell asleep thinking of the hassle of replacing everything in the wallet.

The next morning, I had been up for less than an hour when a man called. Bob identified himself with United Airlines, and his question was music to my ears — "Mr. Blumberg, are you missing a wallet?" Relieved and grateful, I responded, YES! I thanked him for returning my call to United's lost-and-found. But he didn't know about that call. He wasn't with the lost-and-found — nor was it his job to personally follow-up with passengers leaving their stuff on the airplane. He was the night mechanic who had simply found the wallet on my assigned seat. Realizing my phone number was not anywhere in my wallet, I immediately appreciated his extra effort of tracking down my home phone number. But that effort was only the beginning of what I was about to experience.

Bob had waited the night to call, assuming I would be sleeping. He told me that he was leaving work at 7:00 a.m. He wanted to know if I would be home so he could deliver my wallet to my house on his way home. After talking logistics for a minute, I realized that he was going over an hour out of his way. But he insisted. I finally got him to agree that I would immediately leave and meet him in a direction near his home. For the next 45-minutes, we both drove towards a common meeting place.

Feelings

We finally met in the parking lot of a commercial building. As I got out of my car to meet this stranger-turned-hero, I introduced myself to Bob. He sported his heavy United Airlines uniform coat made necessary by the cold December morning. He greeted me with a big smile and handed me my wallet. I pulled some cash from my pocket to give him a sizeable tip for all his efforts. As I reached to hand him the cash, he didn't miss a beat. He simply responded, "Absolutely not!"

Bob continued, "I have lost my wallet before and I know it is a hassle. I am just glad that I could get it back to you." Feeling the need to somehow respond to his kindness, I offered the tip a couple more times. But he was not budging. Realizing the tip minimized his graciousness, I just smiled and said, "I guess I will just have to pay-it-forward to someone else." He smiled, "That would be great." You see, Bob went the extra mile…and then some. He didn't do it for gain, he did it simply because it's who he is."

During our Dash on this earth, we all have countless opportunities to perform unexpected acts of kindness. Emerson said it best; "To share often and much…to know even one life has breathed easier because you have lived; this is to have succeeded."

"The true meaning of life is to plant trees under whose shade you do not expect to sit."
— NELSON HENDERSON

Feelings

Anger

"And be less quick to *anger*
and show appreciation more."

Anger

Our emotions are powerful motivators, and more than almost anything else in our lives they will drive our behavior. Sometimes our greatest challenge is to get inside our own heads to understand what make us tick. Why do we feel and behave the way we do?

I know two family members who were best of friends, but several years ago, one reminded the other of something that had happened thirty years earlier. One thing led to another and, you know what, they haven't spoken since.

William Ward identified the cure when he said, "Forgiveness is the key that unlocks the handcuffs of hate."

Those are powerful words, and I know from personal experience…forgiveness works. A few times in my life I've been greatly wronged and taken advantage of. My first reaction, of course, was anger and resentment. I held it for awhile and felt my stomach tie up in knots, my appetite wane, and the joy slip out of my life.

The quote from Ward provided the wake-up call I needed to forgive the person who had wronged me. It was like I had been playing the first half of a basketball game with three-pound steel shoes, and in the locker room the coach said, "Mac, try these new Nikes in the second half." Multiply that by ten and you'll understand how great it feels to unload your "emotional baggage" through the power of forgiveness.

Life is too short to stay angry…even for a day. Just remember that, "this special Dash may only last a little while."

"Forgiveness does not change the past,
but it does enlarge the future."

— PAUL BOESE

Appreciation

Barbara Glanz (www.barbaraglanz.com) is a speaker, author and also a good friend. One of her favorite quotes from Albert Schweitzer is: "Sometimes our light goes out but is blown again into flame by an encounter with another human being. Each of us owes the deepest thanks to those who have rekindled this inner light."

When Barbara speaks, she will ask her audience to shut their eyes and to think about someone who at some time in their lives has rekindled their inner light. She will leave the room in silence for several minutes, and it is always a profound experience for everyone as they remember the JOY they received from the appreciation of someone when they

"And be less quick to anger
and show *appreciation* more."

Appreciation

Afterwards, she'll ask them to write down the name of the person they thought of and to commit to their own act of appreciation by letting that person know in the next 72 hours that they thought of them. She'll suggest a phone call, a note, or even just a little prayer if they are no longer alive.

After one very moving session, a gentleman came up to talk with her and thank her for creating a new awareness in him. He said he had thought of his eighth grade literature teacher because she was everyone's favorite teacher and had really made a difference in all of their lives, and he was going to track her down and let her know what happened.

One afternoon nearly two and a half months later, Barbara received a call from him. He was very emotional on the phone and could hardly get through his story. He said that it had taken him nearly two months to track his teacher down, and when he finally found her, he wrote to her and the following week this was the letter he received back:

Dear John,

You will never know how much your letter meant to me. I am 83 years old, and I am living all alone in one room. My friends are all gone. My family's gone. I taught for 50 years and yours is the first "thank you" letter I have ever gotten from a student. Sometimes I wonder what I did with my life. I will read and reread your letter until the day I die.

He sobbed on the phone. He said, "Every reunion we've had, she is always the one we talked about. She was everyone's favorite teacher – we loved her!"

But no one had ever told her…until she received his letter.*

Never forget…it is not the things you get, but the hearts you touch that will determine your success in your Dash.

"What you leave behind is not what is engraved in stone monuments, but what is woven into the lives of others."

— PERICLES

"And love the people in our lives

like we've never *loved* before."

I recently had dinner with someone who told me that one of his best friends had been killed in a private plane crash, and something happened at the service that he'll never forget. He shared the story with me.

At the memorial service, his friend's wife walked to the podium to speak to the gathering. She said a friend had asked her the best memory she had of their life together. At the moment, she had been too grief-stricken to answer, but she had thought about it since and wanted to answer the question.

They were in their late forties when he died, and she began talking about a time in their life almost twenty years earlier. She had quit her job to obtain her master's degree, and her husband never wavered in his support.

Love

He held down his own job and also did the cooking, cleaning, and other household chores while she studied for her degree.

One time they both stayed up all night. She was finishing her thesis, and he was preparing for an important business meeting. That morning, she walked out on their loft, looked at him over the railing, and just thought about how much she loved him. She knew how important this meeting was to his career, and she was feeling guilty that she didn't even have time to make his breakfast. He grabbed his briefcase and hurried out. She heard the garage door open and close, but much to her surprise, she heard it open again about thirty seconds later. From above, she watched her husband dash into the house and walk over to the neglected coffee table. Tracing his finger through the dust, he wrote the words, "I love you." Then he raced back to his car.

The new widow then looked out at her audience and said, "John and I had a wonderful life together. We have been around the world several times, we've had everything money can buy…but nothing comes close to that moment."

Our Dash moves with lightning speed. It feels like yesterday that I graduated from college…and now thirty-eight years have passed. Although I'm very proud of my business accomplishments, in the end my life comes back to loving and being loved.

Love

~ ❦ ~

"Love may not make the world go around but it sure makes the ride worthwhile."

"Treat each other with *respect*
and more often wear a smile…"

Respect

He was in the Oklahoma City Airport when he saw a woman walking along with three little girls. They were skipping and singing, "Daddy's coming home on a big jet! Daddy's coming home on a big jet!" All excited! Eyes lit up like diamonds! Wild anticipation! They had never before met Daddy coming home on a jet. Their mother was so proud of them and their enthusiasm. You could see it in her eyes.

Respect

Then the plane arrived, the door opened and the passengers streamed in. You didn't have to ask which one was Daddy. The girls' bright eyes were glued on him. But his first look was for his wife and seeing her, he yelled, "Why didn't you bring my top coat?" and walked right past his adoring daughters. Here was a man who had an opportunity to be great, and he didn't recognize it.

Forty years ago, I heard Charlie Cullen tell that story and I never forgot it.

How many times a day, a week, a month, do we have the opportunity to be great through simple acts of kindness? In your Dash, never underestimate the power of a touch, a smile, a kind word, a listening ear, or an honest compliment. All have the potential to turn a life around.

*"How far you go in your life
depends on your being tender with the young,
compassionate with the aged,
sympathetic with the striving, and
tolerant of the weak and strong.
Because someday in your life you will
have been all of these."*

— GEORGE WASHINGTON CARVER

"If we treat each other with respect
and more often wear a *smile*..."

Smile

Smile

Smile

Our Dash is short, but it can be wide:

A bellman made my day recently. After checking into an Atlanta hotel, Sam (his name was on his badge) picked up my two bags, gave a big smile, and said, "Isn't it a gorgeous day today?" I nodded and said, "Sure is." He then said, "I just spent the entire weekend with my two grandkids, and I can't remember when I've had more fun. Aren't kids great?" And then I added, "Sam, it seems like you're having a great day." He then looked up with a grin I'll never forget and said, "Mr. Anderson, every day above ground is a great day!"

I walked into my room feeling recharged by Sam's enthusiasm. It was obvious that he had chosen to live life to the fullest, and given the opportunity to touch someone's life in a positive way, my bet is that he took it, every time.

Every day, we all have that same opportunity to make a positive difference in the lives of others. We can choose to

mope about our lot in life, or we can decide to live in awe, touching hearts along the way.

Ah, yes...we all know ducks who make lots of noise, quacking and complaining about their problems in life. And then there are eagles, who go about their business and consistently soar above the crowd.

Thanks, Sam, for soaring into my life.

"When we choose not to focus on what is missing from our lives but are grateful for the abundance that's present...we experience heaven on earth."

— SARAH BAN BREATHNACH

"So think about this long and hard;
are there things you'd like to *change*?"

~❦~

Change

Change

Over a century ago, William James, one
of the founders of modern psychology,
said "The great discovery of this
generation is that a human being can alter
their life by altering their attitude."
Each day we wake up in the morning, we
choose our clothes, we choose our
breakfast but, most importantly, we
choose our attitudes.

One of the most wonderful things about
having a positive attitude is the number of
people it touches, many times in ways
you'll never know.

Change

In my book, *The Power of Attitude,* I told the story about going to a convenience store to get a newspaper and a pack of gum. The young woman at the check-out counter said, "That'll be five dollars please," and as I reached into my wallet, the thought occurred to me that a newspaper and gum didn't quite make it to five dollars. When I looked up to get a "re-quote," she had a big smile on her face and said, "Gotcha! I got to get my tip in there somehow!" I laughed when I knew I'd been had. She then glanced down at the paper I was buying and said, "I'm sick and tired of all this negative stuff on the front pages. I want to read some good news for a change." She then said, "In fact, I think someone should just publish a Good News newspaper – a paper with wonderful, inspiring stories about people overcoming adversity and doing good things for others. I'd buy one every day!" She then thanked me for coming in and said, "Maybe we'll get lucky tomorrow; maybe we'll get some good news," and she laughed. She made my day.

The following day, after my business appointments, I dropped by the same store again to pick up bottled water, but a different young lady was behind the counter. As I checked out I said, "Good afternoon," and handed her my money for the water. She said nothing – not a word, not a smile…nothing. She just handed me my change and in a negative tone ordered…"Next!"

It hit me right between the eyes: Two people, same age; one made me feel great, and the other, well, made me feel that I had inconvenienced her by showing up.

By the choices we make, by the attitudes we exhibit, we are influencing lives every day in positive or negative ways…our family, our peers, our friends, and even strangers we've never met before and will never meet again. So when you brush your teeth every morning, look in the mirror and ask yourself…"Are there things I'd like to change?" How will you choose to live your Dash…as "the grouch" or as "the good-news girl?" Your answer will go a long way toward determining the joy and happiness that you will experience in your life.

Change

Making a Difference

It's not the things we get but the hearts we touch that will determine our success in life. Making a difference in the lives of others is what the Dash is all about. In the end, however, the significance of our life will be determined by the choices we make. We can choose positive over negative, smiles over frowns, giving over taking and love over hate. It is only when we take responsibility for our choices that we begin to realize we truly are the masters of our fate. Only then will our lives begin to change for the better.

One of the most powerful stories about choices that I've ever read was written by Lance Wubbels in the book we wrote together, *To A Child . . . Love Is Spelled T.I.M.E.* In January of 2003, I sent the title to Lance as a possible gift book idea. Three days later, he wrote this story for the Introduction:

In the faint light of the attic, an old man, tall and stooped, bent his great frame and made his way to a stack of boxes that sat near one of the little half-windows. Brushing aside a wisp of cobwebs, he tilted the top box toward the light and began to carefully lift out one old photograph album after another. Eyes once bright but now dim searched longingly for the source that had drawn him here.

It began with the fond recollection of the love of his life, long gone, and somewhere in these albums was a photo of her he hoped to rediscover. Silent as a mouse, he patiently opened the long-buried treasures and soon was lost in a sea of memories. Although his world had not stopped spinning when his wife left it, the past was more alive in his heart than his present aloneness.

Setting aside one of the dusty albums, he pulled from the box what appeared to be a journal from his grown son's childhood. He could not recall ever having seen it before, or that his son had ever kept a journal. Why did Elizabeth always save the children's old junk? he wondered, shaking his white head.

Opening the yellowed pages, he glanced over a short entry, and his lips curved in an unconscious smile. Even his eyes brightened as he read the words that spoke clear and sweet to his soul. It was the voice of the little boy who had grown up far too fast in this very house, and whose voice had grown fainter and fainter over the years. In the utter silence of the attic, the words of a guileless six-year-old worked their magic and carried the old man back to a time almost totally forgotten.

Difference

Entry after entry stirred a sentimental hunger in his heart like the longing a gardener feels in the winter for the fragrance of spring flowers. But it was accompanied by the painful memory that his son's simple recollections of those days were far different from his own. But how different?

Reminded that he had kept a daily journal of his business activities over the years, he closed his son's journal and turned to leave, having forgotten the cherished photo that originally triggered his search. Hunched over to keep from bumping his head on the rafters, the old man stepped to the wooden stairway and made his descent, then headed down a carpeted stairway that led to the den.

Opening a glass cabinet door, he reached in and pulled out an old business journal. Turning, he sat down at his desk and placed the two journals beside each other. His was leather-

bound and engraved neatly with his name in gold, while his son's was tattered and the name "Jimmy" had been nearly scuffed from its surface. He ran a long skinny finger over the letters, as though he could restore what had been worn away with time and use.

As he opened his journal, the old man's eyes fell upon an inscription that stood out because it was so brief in comparison to other days. In his own neat handwriting were these words:

Wasted the whole day fishing with Jimmy. Didn't catch a thing.

With a deep sigh and a shaking hand, he took Jimmy's journal and found the boy's entry for the same day, June 4. Large scrawling letters pressed deeply in the paper read:

Went fishing with my dad. Best day of my life.

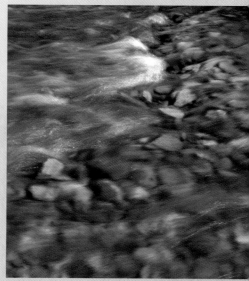

Making

You may have heard it before but it bears repeating. Someone once said, "I've never known anyone who, on their deathbed said…I wish I had spent more time at the office."

Our Dash is a fleeting moment in time, and what we do with it is up to us. The quote on the Priorities print from Successories says it all:

"A hundred years from now it will not matter what my bank account was, the sort of house I lived in, or the kind of car I drove…but, the world may be different because I was important in the life of a child."

The Dash

While it still amazes me, a simple poem I wrote one afternoon forever changed my life. It all began when I faxed a copy of this poem to a syndicated radio show in Atlanta. Soon after receiving it, the host of this popular show read it on the air. Little did I know how much my life would change from that day forward. Titled *The Dash,* these 36 lines have touched millions of lives and have literally taken on a life of their own by traveling all over the world. I call it uncomplicated poetry in a complicated world, which became the slogan for my Internet poetry company, www.lindaellis.net.

People are always asking me what, in particular, inspired me to write this poem. I believe it was a combination of things in my life at the time. It was during a period when I was working for the top executives of a very large and successful corporation. It was a strict company with a tense working environment.

I began to watch how the priorities in many lives there had become misaligned. It seemed to me that the bosses were worrying far too much about that which was inconsequential in the scope of life.

Also, resonating in the back of my mind were the words from a letter which had been previously routed around the office. It had been written by the wife of an employee who was aware that she was dying. I was so moved by that letter that I saved a copy of it and continue to live by her words:

Regrets? I have a few. Too much worrying. I worried about finding the right husband and having children, being on time, being late and so on. It didn't matter. It all works out and it would have worked out without the worries and the tears.

If I would have only known then what I know now. But, I did and so do you. We're all going to die. Stop worrying and start loving and living.

Her words stuck with me. Her letter made me stop and think. This is it. This is all we get.

I remember where I was when I first truly realized the significance of the piece that I had written. I was on a business trip in Minnesota, alone in a hotel room. I received an emotional email thanking me for sharing the message of the Dash from a student who had recently heard it as part of a memorial gathering for the Columbine High School students. I sat on the bed and cried.

Several years later, I found myself engulfed in the thoughts and feelings created by my own words as I listened to them read aloud, for what seemed like the very first time, at the funeral of my father…my best friend. I write this closing exactly one year from that day and never have the words of the poem meant more to me.

From being performed in an elementary
school play somewhere in the heartland of
America to being part of a State Supreme
Court Justice's speech, from being printed
in best-selling novels to high school
yearbooks, *The Dash* has truly affected
millions. I may not be able to change the
world with these words, but I have
certainly been able to influence a portion
of it! The poem's words have convinced

mothers to spend more time with their children, fathers to
spend more time at home, and reunited long-lost loved ones.

The words have changed attitudes, and changed the
direction of lives. They have, in their own way, made a
difference. I know writing *The Dash* has changed my life.
I hope reading it, in some way, may change yours.

Live Your Dash,

Linda Ellis

The Dash

The Power of The Dash:
Our Readers Share Their Stories

"*Things that matter*

most must never be at the mercy of things

that matter least."

~ GOETHE

The Punctuation to Focus On

By David Fell

I was introduced to *The Dash* at, of all places, a corporate meeting. It was meant to be an inspirational coda to a day of sales lectures, business plans and speakers sending the message of motivation to a roomful of more than 200 sales people. As it stands the only thing that stood the test of time from that day-long meeting was the inspiring prose of this poem.

As a man in his forties who has faced the deaths of his parents and childhood best friend, I had become hardened and less enthusiastic about my own life despite the wonderful blessings of my wife and children. Prior to my introduction to *The Dash* I had been inwardly focused on that number after the dash. To be honest, the dash was just a punctuation…nothing more.

Outwardly I would talk the talk of focusing on the good times when the subject of my parents or my best bud, Bob, was mentioned, but inwardly, I was still lamenting about what could have been. I thought about the fact that my dad never got to see his only child marry and have two beautiful, smart and caring grandchildren who he could have told about his years in India in WWII or with whom he could have shared his kind and loving humor. My mom would be unable to see her little granddaughter move up the ranks in gymnastics.

Most of all I pitied the date of 1990 on Bob's tombstone. Bob was ravaged by cancer, dying at the tender age of 25. We were buds since first grade with big plans. College was over, careers were looming, life was "starting." But all that halted and I was devastated, wondering what could have been.

At the conference, when our managing director said that he wanted to share a poem that meant a lot to him, I began to think, "OK let's get on with it." I have at least an hour and ten minute commute home. My mind was focused on the drive and curiosity if the weather was clear. He mentioned the title, *The Dash* and something inside said—listen, focus. Those words rained on me like a wave of redemption. I listened, intently. I was inspired. I was relieved of pity. I was happy. I understood.

I was enlightened. *The Dash* clarified what I was missing—the honor and privilege of the gift I had, not the trauma of what I had lost. I began to smile, realizing the Dash I had with these most important people in my life is what molded me into the person I portrayed outwardly but sorrowed about inwardly. *The Dash* cleansed my soul; it clarified my grieving and changed my perspective on death.

Now the thoughts of what was—the glories and gifts of the lives that so touched me and laid the foundation of my being—are what fill my heart and my mind's eye. I realize that this line, this punctuation, this LIFE is what permeates my being. The numbers on either side are just mile-markers. It is the DASH that I concentrate on.

"A tree is known by its fruit; a man by his deeds.

A good deed is never lost; he who sows courtesy

reaps friendship, and he who plants

kindness gather love."

~ Saint Basil

Benji's Dash

By Gail Blanton

Losing a child is the hardest thing any parent can face. But for one mother, "The Dash" is now the promise of the future for the next generation.

On November 18, 2002, my son, Benji, lost his life in an automobile accident. He was only 27 years old. An umpire and a member of the Green Sea Floyds Recreation (GSF) Department, Benji loved working with the youth of our Green Sea South Carolina community. A few weeks after we lost our son, one of the board members from the GSF Recreation Department called to tell us that the board had decided to set up a scholarship in Benji's memory and to have a monument made for the foot of the flag pole at the recreation department. We were so stunned that they thought so much of Benji to honor his memory in this way.

Six months later, my family and I were sitting in the audience at the Green Sea Floyds Athletic Awards Program where my daughter, Jill, was to present the first Benji Blanton Memorial Scholarship to a senior athlete.

Before Jill went up to present the award, the athletic director of our school, Doug Hinson, read a poem to us. It was *The Dash*. I sat there with tears in my eyes, along with most of the audience.

Making a Difference

When he finished, he said, "Those of you who knew Benji know his Dash was well lived."

When I got home, I put a copy of *The Dash* in a scrapbook I had started with all the memorials of Benji. I would go back often and read it again and again. During the past few years, I have given copies of the book, *The Dash*, to friends who needed to hear this most inspiring and wonderful poem at a time when they were grieving for a loved one.

But, the book also touches the next generation as well. Each year, from now on, each person who receives Benji's scholarship will receive a copy of Linda Ellis' book, *The Dash*.

I have been touched by the poem, *The Dash*, in so many ways. It made me stop and think about life like never before. It has made a huge difference in my life.

Losing my son is the hardest thing I have faced in my life, but with the help of family and friends, I live every day as if it's my last. I am so proud of my son, Benji, and how he lived his Dash. I have been trying to live so that when my eulogy is read, I hope my family will be proud of how I lived mine as well.

"Each of us will one day be

judged by our standard of life,

not by our standard of living;

by our measure of giving,

not by our measure of wealth;

by our *simple goodness,*

~ ❧ ~   not by our seeming greatness."

~ WILLIAM ARTHUR WARD

Uplift Those Around You

by James R. Bowman, MD, ND

When I discovered *The Dash*, I knew intuitively that I held a rare and precious treasure, a great blessing in my hands, but that there were many in the world whose hearts and minds needed to be touched, uplifted and healed by that message. I ordered two cases of *The Dash*, thinking at first, they would make special gifts for special people. Then it began to work on me in a profound way, and I began giving them to everyone. Why? Because my own vision was uplifted and clarified, and I realized that I didn't know anyone who was not a special person deserving of a special gift.

I began giving them only to our sickest patients, then to all patients, the people in our complex ... to everyone. I walked out to the mail box outside as the mailman delivered our letters and I gave him one. The response across the board was huge, ear-to-ear grins and genuine gratitude before they had even opened the book to the first page.

There is something electric in just handing the book to some-one—when they hold it in their hands there is some subtle transfer of synergy that uplifts them.

I love Emerson's quote… "One of the most beautiful compensa-tions in life is that one can never help another without helping himself." That is what happened to me by sharing *The Dash*.

"You can't live a *perfect day* without doing something for someone who will never be able to repay you."

~ JOHN WOODEN

Making the Most
OF YOUR DASH

By Tom Cain

❦

"There is no happiness
in having or in getting,
but only in *giving*."

~ HENRY DRUMMOND

When I first heard *The Dash* at a real estate convention in 2003, it touched my heart. Little did I know how much it would change my life.

Whether I recited *The Dash* at my own father's eulogy or at the end of every speech I make at a business conference, I realized that whatever you do for a living, it's more important what you are doing for your life…and for others. And that's what I am determined to do with my Dash.

Twenty-five years ago, my wife, Sonna, and I started an organization called *Friends of Santa* to bring Christmas cheer to needy families. Over the years, my wife would call each parent or guardian to see what toys their children wanted most. I then dressed the part of Santa and we personally delivered the toys on Christmas Eve. I've heard from the children who I've played "Santa" to over the years, some telling me that it was the best memory of their childhood.

Things began to change with the economy the last few years… for me personally as well. I'm a realtor in Champaign, Illinois, and the last four years have been the worst of my life. I've always been an optimist, but my own Dash got very dim as we struggled just to keep going.

But, despite our economic troubles, my wife and I decided to continue the *Friends of Santa*. And things began to take an interesting turn. As we made calls to the families, we began to hear. "It's nice to give my kids some toys, but we don't have much food and we need some clothes."

My wife called schools and churches and the lightly-used clothing we needed began to come in abundance. With my muscular dystrophy, we made a change in how we deliver the Christmas gifts. Now, instead of "Santa" going out to the families, they come to the Masonic Lodge. One woman stood out in my mind as she brought her children to visit "Santa."

She came in a badly ripped coat. When my wife initially offered her a coat from the clothes we collected, the woman said "no thank you, I'm here for my children"—the way any good parent would. But my wife persisted, saying that we had an abundance of coats and she thought the woman might just like to look.

The woman found a coat for work and a coat for church. In addition, she was given three large leaf-sized bags of clothing—one for each of her children as well as some toys for each child.

The woman was getting ready to leave when I gave her a frozen turkey with all the trimmings. You see, after my dad had passed away from lung cancer, celebrating Christmas was hard for my mom after being married for 50 years. But she decided that, in memory of my father, she was going to buy turkey and the trimmings for the families that needed them most.

The woman was overwhelmed and asked unbelievably, "Is this all mine?" We carried the bags out to old van and after hugging and thanking us, she began to cry with gratitude.

What I've learned from *The Dash*, especially during the last few years, is that when stress and depression come because you are losing material things, it's just stuff…it's not important. What is *important* is that the best way to help ourselves is to help others. That's what living your Dash is really all about.

The Dash Pact

By Laura Quinn

My husband, Andy, became a fan of *The Dash* the first time he read it. It really summed up his attitude toward life...to put family first and live a good life. In March 2009, my sister, Chris, was diagnosed with advanced ovarian cancer. She was 44 at the time. The news was devastating, and the prognosis did not include a cure. My husband admired her spirit and fortitude and told her that if he ever received a devastating diagnosis, he hoped he would have the grace and dignity to face it as optimistically as she did.

Four months later, Andy was diagnosed with acute myelogenous leukemia (AML), and life was forever altered. During their battle with cancer, my sister and husband made a pact. Knowing that they might not survive, the pact became that whoever lived would read *The Dash* at the other's funeral. This was a pact they kept to themselves. In May 2010, ten months after his diagnosis, my husband died. In the course of funeral planning, others had offered to read *The Dash*, but Chris knew she had to keep her promise. Courage takes so many forms. I thought she had incredible courage dealing with her cancer, but I knew for her to read this poem aloud would take emotional courage that few in her situation would be able to muster.

When she stepped to the podium at Andy's funeral mass, we had someone standing by to take over for her in the event she could not finish, but she did not fail. She told the story of the pact in the small chapel of our church. Everyone there knew of her illness, but now they saw her strength. As she read *The Dash*, each word seemed to resonate more than the last—a woman with a terminal illness paying homage to her brother-in-law by keeping their pact. I believe everyone in that church heard *The Dash* as she read it, but her actions expressed the true meaning of *The Dash*—to make each moment, no matter how big or small count—because no one knows how long their Dash will be.

" *Courage*
is not the towering oak
that sees storms come and go,
it is the fragile blossom that
opens in the snow."

~ Alice Mackenzie Swaim

~ ❦ ~

Transformed by The Dash

By Michelle Landahl

I'm just an 18-year-old girl, but this year I experienced tragedy that many people may never experience.

Freshman year, my best friend since kindergarten, Allison "Wonderland" Rivera (nicknamed because of her love of literature) and I took creative writing together, and my teacher gave us *The Dash* to analyze. We both loved it so much… and I held onto that original copy.

I feel like I've known Allie my entire life. She knew me better than I knew myself. She was my crutch, my love, my light… I commonly referred to myself as Frodo and to her as my Samwise Gamgee: the person I could call no matter what the situation and know that she would help, no matter what the cost.

In 2011, I lost my grandpa, the first person close to me who died. I never knew what death really destroyed in people, since I had felt loss but not grief. But on October 15, Minooka Community High School lost a beloved senior, Mitch Fajman,

to Lake Michigan's turbulent waters. He was an acquaintance and our school united to comfort each other. I felt for them. But exactly one week later, I learned exactly what his friends experienced.

I got a call on October 22 from Allie's uncle. She had died instantly from an extremely rare heart defect. She had just turned 18 a month before and finished applying to college. Devastated cannot begin to describe the heart-rending agony I felt. I had to face a school full of questioning eyes and whispers as "Allie's friend" in the days following this tragedy.

But throughout her many memorial services, I sort of became her spokesperson. Even though I was the shy writer, I seemed to be the only one who had the right words to say.

Since Allie's death, I have grown close to her family and I still pay her mom visits to keep her company and fill the void left by the loss of her wonderful daughter.

The first time I went into Allie's house after her death, her face decorated every inch of the home. On the dining room table, next to her senior picture, was a piece of paper I vaguely recognized. When I got closer, I realized that the poem framed next to her smile was the worn and folded copy of *The Dash* we had both received nearly four years ago. I took out her prayer card from my pocket and unfolded my original copy that I had wrapped around it. Her mother burst into tears. We both saved it and neither had known.

When accepting her award for "Best Smile" at our Senior Banquet, I read the first stanza of *"The Dash"* and based my entire speech off it. People have approached me since and told me that those words brought them comfort and changed the way they were planning on living their lives.

I have transformed from the silent, meek girl Allie first met into a leader and a person who I love almost as much as I loved Allie. Allison didn't know how short her Dash was going to be, but one day she looked at me and said, "Michelle, life is short. We shouldn't be afraid to sprint."

It's important not to save all your energy for the final lap; Live your Dash so hard it will be impossible to forget. Don't shut your eyes to the world; you might miss a miracle right in front of you.

"Do not save your loving speeches for
your friends till they are dead.

Do not write them on their tombstones;
speak them now instead."

~ Anna Cummins

WORDS WORTH THEIR

Weight in Gold

By John F. Pilgrim

When I read the poem, *The Dash*, and watched the short movie that accompanied the poem, I was immediately moved. I was determined to share the poem with my friends and co-workers. Fortunately I worked in a senior role with a direct influence on hundreds of pharmacy managers, pharmacists, and health professionals for the largest non-profit HMO in the world, and before I was done, all of them heard and read *The Dash*.

I shared with every manager that they could not effectively lead unless they knew who they were and why they served others, and I selected *The Dash* as the inspiration that allowed me to serve in the way I did. I gave hundreds of copies of *The Dash* to managers, doctors, and pharmacists alike. Every time a gift was given, I explained my daily ritual of watching *The Dash* and then taking about 30 minutes to pray and meditate before really starting my day. I wanted all to know that I just didn't show up in a cheerful optimistic mood. My day was governed by preparation to make sure my daily "dash" was good for me and affected others positively.

Making a Difference

Over the years, I watched the service scores rise and rise, and I believe much of this improvement was nurtured by individuals who realized that they made a difference in the lives of those around them. I was proud to witness people grow at work, and that growth followed them into their homes.

I retired in late 2009, and those who worked with me sent hundreds of e-mails a month telling me of things they have done positively for others. I came out of retirement in October of 2011, and have a daunting job in front of me as I try to build a team of professional winners in a new pharmacy environment.

One of the first things I did was to buy every new pharmacist a copy of *The Dash* and told them if they want to know how I think, to please read the book, BUT more importantly, to read it for themselves, because it would improve their lives.

The Dash is so moving that when others stop to hear it, their lives are literally changed. Mine was. It has helped me have a vision of what is important and what isn't, and has made me realize how we all interact with others as we progress on this journey of life. Words that provide loving direction are worth their weight in gold.

"You come to the planet with nothing

and you leave with nothing,

so you'd better do *some good*

while you're here." ~ 🦋 ~

~ ALEX VAN HALEN

Inspiring Others
TO LIVE THEIR DASH

By Mark Burek

I first heard *The Dash* while attending my dad's retirement ceremony approximately fifteen years ago. The words immediately resonated with me and became my mantra. I live by them daily and share their inspiration with friends and family alike. It's my guideline to living a full life and providing inspiration to others.

I served in the United States Navy for 21 years, retiring in 1998 as a Senior Chief Petty Officer. My tours of duty included deployment to Operation Desert Shield and two tours in Operation Desert Storm. I have three sons who have matured into wonderful young men. My wife is the pillar of the house I call my legacy.

My story begins about halfway through my own Dash. In 2008, at the age of fifty, I was diagnosed with Young Onset Parkinson's Disease. It's a disease which impacts so many aspects of a person's daily routine, from sleep to the simple task of buttoning a shirt. There is no cure for this disease and its progression varies depending upon the individual. I work for the United States Postal Service as a letter carrier and the disease impacts my job greatly. Getting through each day is a challenge. Upon receiving the devastating diagnosis, I immediately read everything I could about this disease and how to fight it. As Rocky Balboa said, "Fighters Fight." I quickly learned that a positive attitude about the disease is essential because no matter how hard you fight, the disease is relentless.

You must live each day to its fullest regardless of how hard the disease attacks your muscles, speech, balance, motor skills etc. The countless days I awaken with pain in my legs and arms are numerous. However, as my feet hit the floor, I thank God for the strength and courage to continue my Dash. Some days are better than others, but each one is a challenge.

As I battled the disease, I realized that there was something missing from my purpose (my Dash). Was I doing my part in battling the disease for others?

In the fall of 2011, I formed Parkinson's Albany, an organization which raises funds and awareness for both education and research in the fight against Parkinson's. With the help of volunteers, we are fighting the fight of our lives. In 2012, I teamed up with the Brian Grant Foundation and we held our first annual Run For Parkinson's fundraiser. What made this event so special was the number of people who wrote letters of thanks to me, telling me how the event has impacted their lives. What was missing in my Dash has been replaced by a desire to inspire people to live their Dash as fully and completely as I live mine. What many may consider a disease, I have turned into a blessing. If I can touch one life each and every day, helping mend a wounded soul, then my Dash will become my instruction for living life fully and completely.

"Enjoy the *little things*,

for one day you may look back

and realize they were the big things."

~ ROBERT BRAULT

Making a Difference

Making Your Dash Matter

By Rob Klinger

Since 1996, I have been blessed to be a volunteer with Hospice of Central Ohio and Compassion In Action, serving mostly veterans at VA Hospitals and in central Ohio.

One of the services Hospice of Central Ohio provides is called "Life Review." It's a process that allows patients to find meaning and purpose in their lives through reflection on their life experiences. In the Life Review, trained volunteer staff members conduct "interviews" with patients upon request, and record these stories digitally.

As a Life Review volunteer, I've had the privilege of sitting across from many individuals who, through the storytelling process, came to realize that the most important dimensions of their lives are focused on faith, family, and friends.

After reading Linda Ellis' poem, *The Dash*, I began to share it with the families of the patients I worked with, and their reaction was consistent: They expressed gratitude for all that God had given them, realized that time is precious, and began working on making a difference with their "Dash."

Recently, I had a conversation with one surviving family member, to whom I had given a copy of *The Dash*. She told me it inspired both her and her family to reflect on their own lives. "I know I must slow down, be grateful for everything, forgive, love more and give without expectation while living my Dash," she said. "We don't have much time here on Earth and I want my Dash to matter."

"We are here to change the world with small acts of *thoughtfulness* done daily rather then with one great breakthrough."

~ RABBI HAROLD KUSHNER

A Dash of Reconnection

By Ralph Olsen

When *The Dash* was first published, I had served as a pastor for 30 years. It was a powerful poem with a message that spoke to my heart. In supporting families who had suffered a death, I often found they had difficulty remembering their loved one's life, so I began to read the poem to them which seemed to help them recall fond memories and events.

It's one thing to help others in their grieving; it is another matter when grief hits you. My father died last October at the age of 89. Our relationship had been strained for many years because he was an alcoholic.

After my mother's death in 1993, the counselor told me to be ready for my father when he came for support. I would have to decide whether I would let him into my life or not. I struggled with the decision, but realized no matter what I had experienced, he was still my father and I was his son. I turned to *The Dash* and read it many times, looking for guidance in my new relationship.

Certain phrases poured into my heart … *are there things you'd like to change … you never know how much time is left … be less quick to anger, show appreciation more, love the people in your life like you've never loved before, remembering that this special dash might only last awhile.* I delivered the eulogy at my dad's memorial service because I knew him best and I was proud of the things I could say about him that were lost in the brokenness of our relationship those many years. Finally, I could say "thank you" dad for spending some of your Dash with me!

" *Forgiveness* is a gift you give yourself."

~ Suzanne Somers

Changing the Lives
OF THOSE AROUND YOU

By Jim Jones

When we lost my wife's nephew, Keith, to brain cancer at age 9, I interviewed those who knew him best. His principal had lost his wife to cancer. He was so affected by Keith's struggle that he resigned to become a grief counselor. Keith's mother went back to college and became a pediatric nurse and his brother decided to become a physician. The way Keith faced his illness and his death greatly inspired others. His Dash was short but impactful.

I also gave a copy of *The Dash* to the mother of an airman, Adam, who drowned in a canoe accident. At his eulogy I recounted the ways he had influenced others. He was a man with a servant's heart—always helping others. His Dash was full of wonderful testimonies. A friend of his, a member of the Corp of Cadets at Texas A&M University, recounted how he was going to quit after his freshman year. But Adam took off work and drove the young man around for three hours, inspiring

him to stick it out. The young man did and is now completing his senior year and will be commissioned as an officer.

When sharing his story at Adam's funeral, the young man said, "I never got to tell Adam thank you. I would have made a big mistake quitting. So now I want to say, "Thank you Adam."

The Dash provides a comforting perspective to a loss. It reminds us all to value our lives and to consider the impact we are having on others. I have been challenged to live my Dash with intentionality. I am pursuing my dream and passion. I want my Dash to inspire others to do the same. I want to hear, "Well done my good and faithful servant" when my Dash is over. Until then, I will give *The Dash* to those who need its message.

"Sometimes *one choice*

not only changes the direction of our lives,

but that of many, many others."

The Power of the Present

By Loryn Halperin

Recently, I was hospitalized for a whole month. During that time, I kept thinking of the "what ifs and the whys"— of how I was when I was healthy and about what would be. I truly gave very little thought to the time I had at that very moment. The Dash between the time I was injured to the time I would leave the hospital became less significant to me. That is … until a nurse reminded me that the most important time you have right now is this moment. Going over the past would not heal me and anticipating the future would not heal me. The present moment—the Dash in between—is the most important time

of a person's life! And then I remembered the book I purchased called *The Dash* and asked my husband to bring it to me from home. I read it over and over again and realized that I needed to worry about the time in-between—my Dash!

Looking back at that month, I learned a lot, even though I was suffering and in pain … not knowing what my future would bring.

My mom, Estelle Glazer, passed in 2005 and she was born in 1935. While her tombstone lists those dates, there was so much more to her. The Dash in-between was about a very warm, loving mother who was there for me when I needed her. It was about her LIFE and how she lived it in the present moment. That is what I learned from *The Dash* and I share it with my friends, family and in the groups I run for Healing Circles. It is truly wonderful and has taught me a lot about myself and how I live my life NOW!

"Celebrate the happiness that friends are always giving;

Make every day a holiday and

celebrate just living"

~ AMANDA BRADLEY

A Dash of Forgiveness

By Delores West

After reading *The Dash* I realized that it really doesn't matter when you were born or when you die. I started asking myself what is my purpose and I realized that I was going to start living my Dash. At that very moment, my life began to change. Every chance I get I try to make other people happy. I get so much enjoyment looking at their faces at the end of the day knowing that it comes from the heart.

When I visited Jamaica, I started thinking about how I was living compared to the lives of some of the Jamaicans. At that moment I wished I had enough money to share with all of them and I began to cry. I knew that I couldn't change things for all of them but I could rearrange my day and make someone happy, which happened to be the young lady who was taking care of my room. *The Dash* made me care for others as if they were family. I went to the front desk and asked for her, thanked her for her service and gave her a gift. You would have thought I gave her a million dollars. She came back to hug me over and over again and asked me if I was sure about the amount. I said I was sure and that I wished it could have been more.

The Dash also changed my ability to forgive. I was hurt by friends of more than 20 years. After reading *The Dash* about "Anger," I realized that life is too short to stay angry and hurt. Forgiveness doesn't change the past, but it did change my life. *The Dash* made me realize that you can't change people; you have to accept them the way that they are or leave them alone.

I started trying to be around positive people. When I find myself beginning to feel out of sorts, I read *The Dash* and it pulls me back to reality.

I now enjoy every second of my life. Thank you Mac Anderson and Linda Ellis for opening up my eyes to life and for making me realize what that Dash means to me.

"All that is worth cherishing in this world begins in the *heart,* not in the head."

~ Suzann Chapin

A Dash Just Started

By Darin Mott and Rachel Venefra

As a 7th grade English teacher for more than 20 years, Darin Mott ends each school year with an inspirational message to his classes about the importance of making a difference in the lives of others. He gives each student a card with a message … and a challenge. The message on the card is "One stone can change the complexion of an entire pond … one heart can change the complexion of an entire world." The challenge is for students to return with their cards at the end of their 8th-grade year and again at the end of their senior year of high school. If they do, he has a gift for them—a copy of *The Dash*.

"This book has been such an important reminder to me of the value of each day and the work I get to do with kids," said Mott. "Last year, one of my former students, Rachel Venefra, shared a powerful letter with me about how a medical condition caused her to re-evaluate her Dash at age 17."

> *Dear Mr. Mott,*
>
> *Thank you for not only being an amazing teacher, thank you for changing my life, and helping me see things differently. On August 2nd, I became sick. I couldn't eat. I could barely walk, and all I could do was sleep. My mom thought it was the flu, but it got worse and I went to the ER.*
>
> (But Rachel's illness didn't go away and when her eyes started to cross, she saw a neurologist. An MRI confirmed that she had a blood clot in her brain.)
>
> *I was so weak. I couldn't walk at all and my heart rate would jump to 160 beats/minute when I stood up. I was put on a heart monitor and was in the hospital for eight long days.*

No 17-year-old should have to go through this. Now, I can walk but my hands are numb. I still have crossed eyes because of the clot. The doctor said my eyes will get better in a few months.

No matter what I went through, I kept a good attitude. I'm so happy to be alive. One in four million people get this kind of clot. Lucky, huh?

I didn't read "The Dash" until I got home from the hospital. I bawled my eyes out. Life really is short. You never know what could happen. I wanted to thank you for that book. It has helped me a lot through this long recovery.

Please don't take life for granted. Every hour of every day is a miracle. The words in "The Dash" are definitely words to live by. Thank you again for everything.

Sincerely,

Rachel Venefra

P. S. Life is never really that bad. Every day you can wake up, is automatically a good day. I'm making my Dash a good one.

Update from Rachel:

Everything is back to normal for me. All of my feeling has come back and my vision is perfect. I'm now off my blood thinners and living a much easier life. I got another CT scan and I still have three small clots but they are nothing to worry about. It feels amazing to be healthy again!

"As we express our *gratitude,*

we must never forget that the highest appreciation

is not to utter words, but to live by them."

~ JOHN F. KENNEDY

MAC ANDERSON

MAC ANDERSON is the founder of Simple Truths and Successories, Inc., the leader in designing and marketing products for motivation and recognition. These companies, however, are not the first success stories for Mac. He was also the founder and CEO of McCord Travel, the largest travel company in the Midwest, and part owner/VP of sales and marketing for Orval Kent Food Company, the country's largest manufacturer of prepared salads.

His accomplishments in these unrelated industries provide some insight into his passion and leadership skills. He also brings the same passion to his speaking where he speaks to many corporate audiences on a variety of topics, including leadership, motivation, and team building.

Mac has authored or co-authored twenty-two books that have sold over three million copies. His titles include: *Change is Good … You Go First, Charging the Human Battery, Customer Love, Finding Joy, Habits Die Hard, Leadership Quotes, Learning to Dance in the Rain, 212°: The Extra Degree, 212° Service, 212° Leadership, Motivational Quotes, One Choice, The Best of Success, The Nature of Success, The Power of Attitude, The Power of Kindness, The Essence of Leadership, The Road to Happiness, The Dash, To a Child, Love is Spelled T-I-M-E, You Can't Send a Duck to Eagle School, What's the Big Idea?*

For more information about Mac, **visit www.simpletruths.com**

LINDA ELLIS

Linda Ellis started writing creatively as a child, a talent inherited from her Irish grandmother. She grew up in Florida and then moved to New York for several years. However, her southern roots kept calling her home and she settled in Georgia where she now lives with her family.

She spent many years working in the corporate environment, but after her first poem was shared on a syndicated radio program in 1994, an alternative career began to emerge and she soon came to the realization that her true passion was writing.

Because no promotion or raise received from her boss could ever equal the satisfaction she felt when she would hear from those whose hearts had been touched by her words, she made the decision to leave the corporate world behind to pursue her dream: inspiring others through her writing and speaking.

Millions of people have been touched by her words and today she shares her inspirations through her company, "Linda's Lyrics." In addition to writing, she is an inspirational speaker and makes a special connection with her audiences through her insightful and thought-provoking presentations.

Simple Truths of Life follows the success of her gift book, *The Dash, Making a Difference with Your Life,* co-authored with Mac Anderson. Her next book, *Every Single Day,* is scheduled for publication in 2011.

For more information about Linda, visit: **www.lindaellis.net**